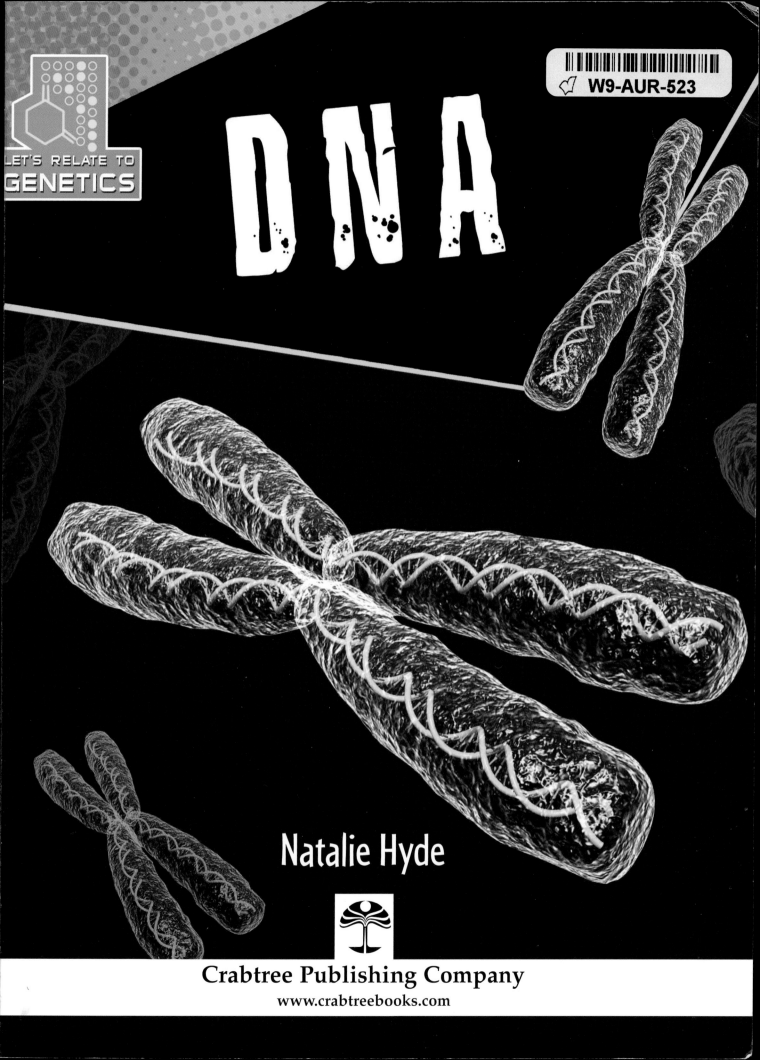

LET'S RELATE TO
GENETICS

DNA

W9-AUR-523

Natalie Hyde

Crabtree Publishing Company
www.crabtreebooks.com

Crabtree Publishing Company

www.crabtreebooks.com

Author: Natalie Hyde
Coordinating editor: Chester Fisher
Series editor: Jessica Cohn
Editorial director: Kathy Middleton
Editor: Adrianna Morganelli
Proofreader: Reagan Miller
Production coordinator: Katherine Berti
Prepress technician: Katherine Berti
Project manager: Kumar Kunal (Q2AMEDIA)
Art direction: Harleen Mehta (Q2AMEDIA)
Cover design: Tarang Saggar (Q2AMEDIA)
Design: Ritu Chopra (Q2AMEDIA)
Photo research: Mariea Janet (Q2AMEDIA)

Cover:
Main image:
    Paired bases, or chemicals, act like the rungs on the
    double helix, or spiral-shaped, ladder of DNA.
Inset image:
    DNA profiling is used to identify victims of accidents,
    to discover members of a family tree, and to study
    genetic diseases.
What makes you the person you are?:
    Deoxyribonucleic acid, or DNA, is the chemical code that
    acts like a set of instructions to your body on how to build
    itself. Your genes are only part of what makes you the person
    you are. Once your body is built, the rest is up to you.

Photographs:
Alamy: Jim Kidd: p. 31
Associated Press: Amr Nabil: p. 39 (top)
BigStockPhoto: p. 23 (bottom); Eraxion: p. 13 (right)
Capital Pictures: p. 25 (right)
Compare Infobase Limited: p.33
Corbis: Bettmann: p. 11 (right); Ann Johansson: p. 36; Rykoff Collection:
    p. 37 (top)
Dreamstime: Eraxion: p. 8
Fotolia: Mark Rasmussen: p. 7
Istockphoto: Yuri Khristich: p. 13 (left); Johnny Scriv: p. 23 (top);
    Chris Schmidt: p. 28; Willem Schulte: p. 38; Istockphoto: p. 42–43
Photographersdirect: Christiano Sant Anna: p. 41
Photolibrary: Sarah Jones: cover (bottom); Photolibrary: p. 9 (bottom);
    Laguna Design: p. 19 (bottom); Scott Camazine: p. 21 (top); London
    Scientific Films: p. 26–27
Reuters: Dani Cardona: p. 25 (left)
Science Photo Library: Pasieka: p. 19 (top)
Shutterstock: Andrea Danti: cover (top); Shutterstock: p. 1, 5 (left),
    6, 9 (top), 35 (top), 39 (bottom), 44, 45; Dimitrios Kaisaris: p. 4;
    Cokeker: p. 5 (right); Benjaminet: p. 10; Mark Gabrenya: p. 11 (left);
    Marek R. Swadzba: p. 12; Peter G: p. 14; Zentilia: p. 15; Jkitan: p. 18;
    Steve Cukrov: p. 20; Javarman: p. 21 (bottom); Sebastian Kaulitzki:
    p. 22; Noam Armonn: p. 24; Adam Majchrzak: p. 27; Jason Maehl:
    p. 30; Felix Mizioznikov: p. 32; Hans Slegers: p. 34; Tony Wear:
    p. 35 (bottom); Tulcarion: p. 37 (bottom); Loren Rodgers: p. 40;
    Oralleff: p. 43
Q2AMedia Art Bank: p. 16–17, 34, 35

Library and Archives Canada Cataloguing in Publication

Hyde, Natalie, 1963-
    DNA / Natalie Hyde.

(Let's relate to genetics)
Includes index.
ISBN 978-0-7787-4948-6 (bound).--ISBN 978-0-7787-4965-3 (pbk.)

    1. DNA--Juvenile literature. I. Title. II. Series: Let's relate to genetics

QP624.H93 2009   j572.8'6   C2009-903884-6

Library of Congress Cataloging-in-Publication Data

Hyde, Natalie, 1963-
    DNA / Natalie Hyde.
        p. cm. -- (Let's relate to genetics)
    Includes index.
    ISBN 978-0-7787-4948-6 (reinforced lib. bdg. : alk. paper) -- ISBN 978-0-7787-4965-3
(pbk. : alk. paper)
    1. DNA--Juvenile literature. I. Title. II. Series.

QP624.H93 2010
572.8'6--dc22

                                    2009024758

Crabtree Publishing Company
www.crabtreebooks.com   1-800-387-7650

Printed in the USA/012014/CG20131129

Published in Canada
Crabtree Publishing
616 Welland Ave.
St. Catharines, ON
L2M 5V6

Published in the United States
Crabtree Publishing
PMB 59051
350 Fifth Avenue, 59th Floor
New York, New York 10118

Published in the United Kingdom
Crabtree Publishing
Maritime House
Basin Road North, Hove
BN41 1WR

Published in Australia
Crabtree Publishing
3 Charles Street
Coburg North
VIC, 3058

Contents

Chapter 1

Blueprint of Life

The tiny living stone cactus and the blue whale have something in common. It's obviously not size. It's not their habitat, favorite meal, or life cycle. It's the same thing that you share with a dung beetle, a Venus fly trap, and a Tyrannosaurus rex.

Deep inside each cell of every living thing (even the extinct ones) are instructions for its shape, size, and texture. These instructions are "written" in a chemical code known as **deoxyribonucleic acid**, or **DNA** for short. The code works like a blueprint. A blueprint is a plan that maps out a building, vehicle, or engine and its dimensions.

The DNA in elephant cells tell the cells to grow a nose long enough to reach the ground. The instructions inside a peach tree know to grow a covering around the tree's seeds. Your DNA tells your body to grow ten fingers and one nose.

If you could see DNA, you could see that it looks like a twisted ladder.

The study of DNA is changing life as we know it.

This chemical code comes in a bundle so small, it fits inside a cell. Yet DNA controls everything about life on Earth. The DNA code can be written in an infinite number of patterns, which has created an amazing diversity of plants and animals on our planet.

If It's Everywhere, Why Can't I Find it?

You would think that instructions for so many parts and so many jobs would be big. Very big! Yet DNA is so small that you cannot see it without a very powerful microscope. How small is this set of instructions? Your entire DNA fits inside a single cell. Thousands of human cells can fit into the period at the end of this sentence.

The reason so much information can fit into such a small space is because of the way DNA is made. If you stretched out the DNA from one cell, it would be a thread about six feet (1.8 meters) long. The thread would be so thin, about five million of them would fit through the eye of a needle. The DNA in a cell is not made in one long, simple strand either. It is divided into pieces of different lengths. These pieces are called **chromosomes**.

Chromosomes, if you could see them, would look like this up close.

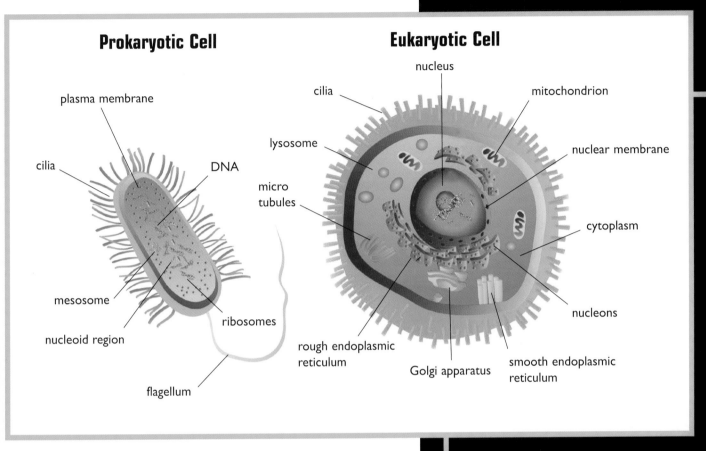

Prokaryotic Cell

plasma membrane

cilia

DNA

mesosome

nucleoid region

ribosomes

flagellum

Eukaryotic Cell

nucleus

cilia

mitochondrion

lysosome

nuclear membrane

micro tubules

cytoplasm

nucleons

rough endoplasmic reticulum

Golgi apparatus

smooth endoplasmic reticulum

The DNA of each chromosome twists and coils until it takes up very little room. All living things have DNA in their cells. Yet different **species** have different numbers of chromosomes. Camels have 70; petunias have 14. Fruit flies have eight, and humans have 46. Chromosomes don't all look the same. The chromosomes stay in a part of the cell called the **nucleus**. The nucleus is like the bank vault of the cell. Walls inside the nucleus, called **membranes**, protect the DNA.

DNA Storage
Bacteria and related organisms are made of prokaryotic cells. Their DNA is found in the nucleoid. Eukaryotic cells are plant and animal cells. Their DNA is found in the nucleus. Their mitochondria also have some DNA.

Chapter 2

Path to Discovery

Early scientists suspected that there was something in the cells that determined the features of living things. Yet it was hard to figure out DNA's role before there were microscopes powerful enough to see it.

Friedrich Miescher, a medical student, was the first to identify what's now known as DNA. In 1869, he found a strange substance inside the nucleus of white blood cells. He named it **nuclein**. Few people took notice, however.

In 1924, a team of researchers used dye on the parts of a cell. The stains helped them see that chromosomes were made of **protein** and DNA matter. These researchers thought that the protein carried genetic instructions. Then Oswald Avery, Colin MacLeod, and Maclyn McCarty experimented with a **virus** and bacteria.

This model shows how a virus (green) attacks a cell (blue).

They stained the protein and DNA of the virus in different colors. They watched as the virus injected its DNA (and not its protein) into the bacteria. This showed that DNA was the active substance. The team published their results in 1944. Suddenly, everyone was interested!

Scientists made **crystals** of DNA, and Rosalind Franklin used x-rays to photograph a DNA crystal. The **molecules** in crystals line up in tight formations. When x-rays hit them, the rays scatter in certain patterns. By studying the patterns, she could figure out the structure of the thing being photographed. The DNA crystal made a pattern that told Franklin that DNA was formed like a **helix**.

James Watson and Francis Crick saw Franklin's work and realized that DNA wasn't a single helix, but a double one. In 1962, Watson and Crick won the Nobel Prize for putting the pieces together.

Rosalind Franklin identified the shape of DNA as a helix.

Eeew! Cells for the Picking
When Friedrich Miescher wanted to study the parts of the nucleus, he needed a supply of cells. He solved his problem by going to a hospital and taking used bandages full of pus. Pus is the yellowy liquid in wounds that are infected. White blood cells fight infection. He knew there would be plenty of white blood cells in the pus.

Chapter 3

The Code of Life

We say that DNA is a blueprint for life. Yet if you look at DNA under a microscope, it does not look like a blueprint. It looks like a single thread that is all bunched up.

If you could look closer, you would see that DNA is more like two threads that form a double helix. A single helix is a curve like the coil on a screw. A double helix is two identical curves that are joined along their middle. A double helix is much stronger than a single helix.

Rungs of a Ladder

DNA looks like a ladder that is twisted around and around. The long sides are made of alternating sugar and phosphate **atoms**. Attached to each of the sugar atoms are different chemicals called **bases**. There are four bases; they are adenine, guanine, thymine, and cytosine. Scientists call them A, G, T, and C for short. Two bases pair up to make the rungs of the ladder.

DNA rungs are made of chemicals called bases. There are two bases on each rung.

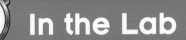

Computers use just two digits in countless combinations. DNA uses four letters.

Scientists did not believe that DNA was the code of life when it was first discovered, because it did not seem possible that so much information could be stored with so few chemicals. Once computers were invented, scientists realized that an astounding amount of information could be stored with only two numbers. A computer uses only the numbers zero and one in different combinations to do all its work. The number of combinations using the four bases is enormous.

The Scoop

When an organism dies, its DNA starts to break into smaller pieces. If the body dries out or freezes, the DNA stops decaying. That is why DNA has been recovered from humans and animals from thousands of years ago. DNA from a mastodon was found in an old tooth. One of the best places to find DNA, however, is in ancient poop. Why? Cells from the intestines of the organism can usually be found in it.

Base Pairs

Every plant and animal on Earth uses the same chemicals to form their DNA. So how is it that we have such a variety of shapes and sizes in nature? Why does a human look so different from a cactus or a salamander? The secret lies in the way the chemicals are put together to make the DNA strands.

The four bases always come in pairs. A always joins with T, and C always pairs with G. The reason for this has to do with the size of each base. When an A and T join, they are the same length as a C and G together. This is important because this keeps all the rungs of the DNA ladder the same size. There are no bumps and bulges in the double helix to make it weak. The pattern of A's, T's, C's, and G's down the sides of the ladder are a building code for the body. It is the different combinations of these bases that make us all look unique.

You share some DNA with a salamander.

DNA combinations can be mapped in diagrams like this.

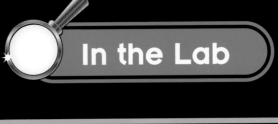

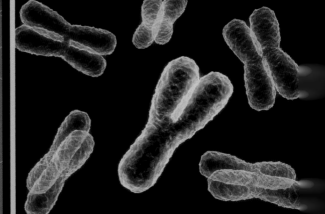

On each chromosome are hundreds of thousands of base pairs. The sections of each chromosome are the code for one special function. Those sections are called **genes**. There are genes for building your heart, for making muscles, for growing your hair, and for determining the color of your eyes.

Did You Know?

Different chromosomes have different numbers of genes on them. Chromosome 1 has the most, about 3,000. The Y chromosome has the least, around 100. Genes can be different sizes, too. Most have an average of 3,000 base pairs. The largest gene is the code for a protein called dystrophin. It is about 2.4 million base pairs long.

Making Copies

Every life starts as a single cell. That cell divides and makes two cells. The two cells divide and make four. This continues until there are thousands or millions of cells. Each one has the identical information ready to create a new plant or animal.

Each time a cell divides, it copies its DNA so that each new cell has the complete blueprints for the body it is helping to build. This is called DNA **replication**. The special double helix shape of DNA makes the copying easy.

A template is a pattern used repeatedly, such as the plans for a robot army. DNA works like a template.

14

How? The first thing the DNA does is untwist so it is flat. Then it breaks apart between the base pairs like a zipper unzips. After the break, the DNA is in two parts. Each has a long strand and a row of single bases down one side. Each side will form the **template** for a new strand of DNA. A template is a pattern or design used repeatedly.

In the nucleus, plenty of extra bases float around. These bases begin to join up with their partners. The A bases join to T bases. T's join to A's. C's join to G's, and G's join with C's. Once all the bases have new partners, the sugar and phosphate molecules link up to make the outer side of the DNA ladder.

The strands twist back up and coil tightly. At that point, there are two exact copies of the DNA making two matching chromosomes. Once all the chromosomes have doubled, the cell nucleus divides down the middle. Each half gets one set of chromosomes.

In the Lab

Believe It or Not!
Even though replication is a complicated process, human DNA speeds along at about 50 bases per second. Still, this is slow compared to bacteria. They can replicate at an incredible 1,000 bases per second!

Bacteria replicate at an alarming rate.

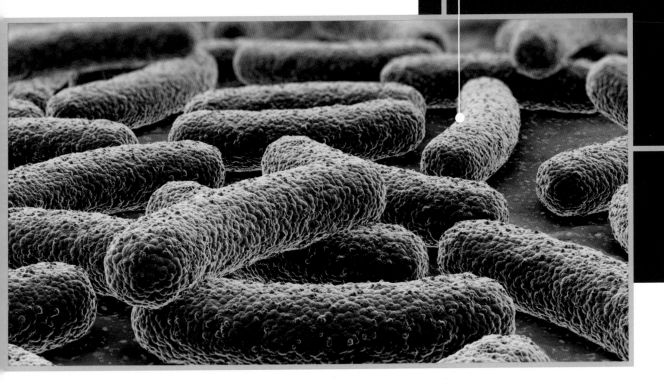

Replicating DNA

Looking at the Ladder
The structure of DNA is a double helix. In this model, the colors on the rungs stand for the bases. See how two bases form each rung and that each rung is the same size. Then look at the image on page 17 to imagine the steps that DNA goes through to replicate itself.

Unzipping DNA

DNA can unzip only when it is untwisted. Replication does not start at one end and work to the other. DNA untwists and unzips at many places along the strand at the same time. This makes replication much faster.

Making an Exact Copy

The extra bases match up with their partners on each half of the unzipped strand. They are held together in the middle by hydrogen molecules. Once the bases are in place, sugar and phosphate molecules form the other side of the strand. In the end, there are two identical strands of DNA.

New Kid on the Block

DNA is the most precious material in any living thing. Without it, limbs wouldn't grow and hearts wouldn't beat. Petals wouldn't form on flowers. The cells protect the DNA in the nucleus. Yet in order for the code to be used, the information has to get from the nucleus out into the cell.

The DNA makes a special copy of itself to do that. Unlike when a cell divides, the whole chromosome does not replicate. Instead only the part that is needed, the specific gene, makes a copy. The new material is called **ribonucleic acid**, or RNA for short. RNA is made from all the same chemicals as DNA except for one. In RNA, thymine is replaced with uracil, or U.

DNA tells plants and animals which traits to express.

When DNA gets ready to make RNA, it untwists the section it needs. Then it unzips so the base pairs separate. In this process only one side of the DNA strand is used as a template. Spare bases join up with their partners. C's still pair up with G's, but A's join with U's. When the strand is complete, the RNA pulls away from the DNA. The DNA zips back up with the other half and twists up again. The single strand RNA is now free to pass through the membrane of the nucleus and head out into the cell where the genetic code will be put to work.

In the Lab

When DNA copies into RNA it is called **transcription**. Transcription and replication are two ways for DNA to make copies.

RNA is structured so it can carry genetic information.

19

Copy That

Once the DNA has copied itself onto the single strand, the RNA slips through holes in the membrane of the nucleus. The RNA heads out into the cell to start its job.

The cell is like a company. Different parts of the cell do different jobs. The DNA is like the boss. It stays in its office, the nucleus, and runs everything. DNA takes signals from other parts of the body, like a boss answering the telephone. That way, the DNA knows what gene it needs to use.

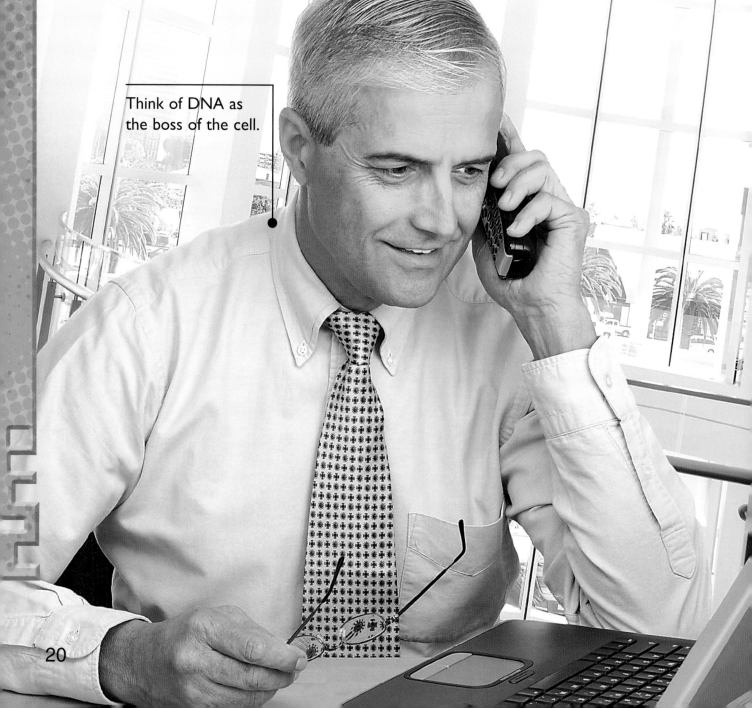

Think of DNA as the boss of the cell.

The strand of RNA that takes the genetic recipe out into the cell is like a messenger service. In fact, scientists refer to it as "messenger RNA" or mRNA for short. This is how the code reaches the **ribosomes** in the main part of the cell.

The ribosomes are the construction workers of the cell. They are called ribosomal RNA, or rRNA. There are a lot of ribosomes floating around in the **cytoplasm**, or fluid part of the cell. The ribosomes wait for instructions. Just as there are extra bases in the nucleus to help DNA replicate and transcribe, materials in the cytoplasm help the rRNA make their proteins. These materials are called **amino acids**. Ribosomes take the code provided by the messenger. They use the code to make long chains of amino acids that look like beaded necklaces.

The genetic instructions are usually very long. The instructions use hundreds or thousands of amino acids. Ribosomes need help to round them up in the cell. This is the job of "translator RNA," also known as tRNA. It brings the amino acids to the rRNA like a delivery truck.

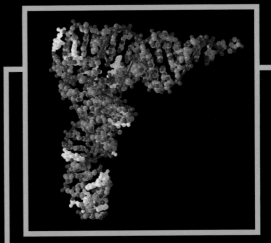

Believe it or Not!
About five to ten percent of the total weight of a cell is RNA. Compare that to DNA, which only makes up about one percent!

Think of the tRNA as a delivery service in the cell.

Antibodies have "arms" that bind to intruding cells.

Make Mine a Protein, Please

Long chains of amino acids do not sound as if they would be very useful in the body. Yet strands of amino acids form proteins if put together properly. Proteins are vital to the body. **Hemoglobin**, for instance, is a protein in our blood. It carries oxygen. **Antibodies** are proteins, too. They fight off viruses and bacteria that invade our bodies. **Enzymes** in our saliva and stomach help break down the food we eat. That way, our bodies can digest the food. Enzymes are another form of protein.

A ribosome connects with a newly formed strand of mRNA. The ribosome begins by reading the list of parts needed, starting with the first three bases. That provides a code for a specific amino acid. Each group of three bases is code for a different amino acid. The groups of three bases are called **codons**. The mRNA is a long grocery list of codons, one after the other.

The minute the ribosome is finished, the lineup of amino acids starts folding. Each protein folds itself into a different shape, which will help it do its job. Sometimes a protein is made from more than one strand of amino acids.

The proteins have different shapes. **Collagen** is a protein which forms tendons to connect our bones. Collagen is long! It is three strands twisted together. Antibodies, which fight diseases, are Y-shaped. The two arms of the antibody bind to the intruder. The base sends signals for help.

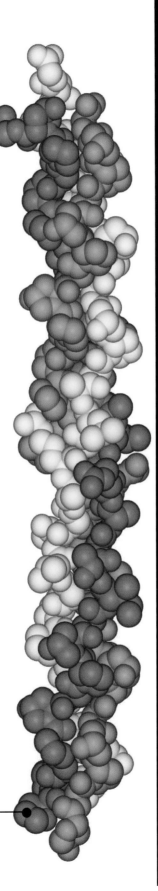

A computer image of collagen shows its twisted form.

Up Close

Here is the beginning of the genetic code for **keratin**. Keratin is the protein that forms our hair and fingernails. It is also the main ingredient in feathers, wool, claws, scales, horns, and hooves.

ATG ACT ACC TGC AGC CGC CAG
TTC ACC TCC TCC AGC TCC ATG
AAG GGC TCC TGC GGC ATC GGG
GGC GGC ATC GGG GCG GGC TCC
AGC CGC ATC TCC TCC GTC CTG
GCC GGA GGG TCC TGC CGC GCC
CCC AAC ACC TAC GGG GGC GGC
CTG TCT GTC TCA TCC TCC CGC
TTC TCC TCT GGG

It would take 50 years of eight-hour days to type your genetic code.

Changes in the Code

It would not be an easy task to type out your own genetic code from all your chromosomes. Typing very quickly for eight hours a day, it would take you about 50 years to finish it.

What would happen if you made a mistake and typed the wrong letter? What if instead of typing ATG you typed ATC? When the ribosome reads that codon, it would string on the wrong amino acid.

Mistakes in replicating or transcribing DNA are called **mutations**. Mutations can happen for many reasons. Radiation from the Sun or x-rays can cause problems in cells. That is why x-ray technicians wear lead padding or leave the room to protect themselves. Polluted air, food, and water contain elements that change or stop chemical reactions in our cells. This can cause problems, too.

During replication, sections of the code can separate and turn around. This causes part of the code to be backward. This is called a **reversal**. Other times sections can be repeated, making the gene too long. This is called an **insertion**. Some errors in the code happen for no reason at all. They are called **spontaneous mutations** because they can happen at any time.

During cell division, problems with chromosomes can cause mutations.

To the Rescue

Mutant superheroes in movies usually have a genetic change that makes them stronger, such as the character Colossus in X-Men. Or they might get other special powers, such as Wolverine's ability to heal. Mutations in nature are not always bad. Sometimes the accidental new protein will help the plant or animal work better or faster. Scientists believe this is how life forms **evolved**.

Missing in Action

Proteins are essential for a body to work properly. They help regulate body systems and move chemicals. They fight infections and help in normal development and growth. If proteins are missing or do not have the right shape, they can cause serious problems.

Hemoglobin helps carry oxygen in the blood. If the gene that makes one of the proteins in hemoglobin is mutated, the person can develop a disease called sickle cell anemia. These crescent-shaped red blood cells do not carry oxygen as well as those with the usual round shape. This can cause problems in the heart, muscles, and all the other organs that need a good supply of oxygen.

Large sections of missing code cause even bigger problems. A three-legged dog may have a deletion in its DNA. The code for growing limbs may be missing. Other deletions on a chromosome may affect the development of the eyes, ears, or brain. This can cause trouble with coordination or learning disabilities.

Compare healthy red blood cells with those with a sickle shape.

Protein Problems

Some people suffer from autism, which is a disorder that causes problems with learning and with interacting with others. People with autism may be missing a protein that helps certain brain cells develop properly. The cells are needed for communication.

People who have Down syndrome are not missing any genetic code. They have more DNA than other people. They have one whole extra chromosome number 21. There are 47 chromosomes in each nucleus in their cells.

No Sugar, Please!
The protein **insulin** helps break down sugar for the body to use for energy. People with diabetes do not make enough insulin in their pancreas. They have to take insulin in pills or injections every day.

Chapter 4

Looking for Answers

What if human beings came with an instruction manual just like the kind that comes with a washing machine? It would explain all the parts of the body. It would teach us how everything worked.

The manual would tell us how to make repairs when parts are damaged. Now imagine that the manual is written in a strange language. This is a language that uses only four letters over and over. In order to be able to read the important information, you have to crack the code.

Your cells contain your DNA code.

Human beings and every other organism on Earth do have an instruction manual. It's our **genome**. A genome is all the DNA from one set of chromosomes. Scientists know that if they can figure out what all the DNA sequences mean, they can unlock some incredible information.

Researchers started sequencing the genomes of different plants and animals. The first thing they discovered was that we all share quite a bit of our DNA. In fact, about 26 percent of our genome is the same as a small plant from the mustard family. We share about 85 percent with the zebra fish. People have 90 percent in common with mice and 99 percent with chimpanzees. We even share 21 percent with the roundworm.

In the Lab

Size of the Situation

Researchers were surprised to discover that genome sizes didn't always match how complex an organism was. They assumed that human beings would have the largest genome. We don't. Here's how we measure up:

Organism	Approx. Number of Base Pairs
yeast	12,100,000
fruit fly	130,000,000
python	1,500,000,000
honeybee	1,770,000,000
humans	3,200,000,000
amoeba	670,000,000,000
salamander	765,000,000,000

Small but Mighty

Some of the smallest living things in the world may hold the biggest secrets. **Microbes** are creatures that can only be seen with microscopes. Microbes can live almost everywhere in the world. They can be found in soil, water, air, rocks, and even in other animals. Some microbes live in hot springs. The water there is so hot it would burn your skin to a crisp in two seconds. Other microbes live happily at the bottom of the ocean. Here, the pressure from the water above would crush you into a blob the size of a soccer ball. Other microbes live in water where they breathe rust instead of oxygen.

Bacteria can survive in hot spring such as this one, in Yellowstone National Park.

How do they do these amazing things? Scientists believe that answers can be found in the DNA of tiny organisms. They are trying to discover the genetic codes that allow microbes to live where they do. Scientists hope to learn new ways to produce fuel or clean up toxic waste by studying the microbes' DNA.

The Next Big Thing

Scientists all around the world are helping with a new project called the Microbial Genome Project. They are mapping the DNA of many new species of microbes. They are also investigating microbe communities to understand how they all work together. Microbes have lived in every imaginable place on Earth for millions of years and may hold clues to how life began on our planet.

Sorcerer II took a two-year global journey, catching microbes for genetic sequencing.

Around the World
The Sorcerer II is a sailboat that was turned into a research lab. The team onboard took samples from the oceans around the globe. They strained the water through several layers of filter paper. This caught microbes, which were frozen and shipped to a laboratory. There, scientists studied the DNA.

Twin studies help us understand how genes work.

Twin Studies

Every living thing has a unique set of DNA with one exception. Identical twins (or triplets) share the same genetic code because they grow from the same fertilized egg cell. Fraternal twins have different DNA because they grow from two different fertilized eggs.

Studying identical twins is helpful to medical researchers. Identical twins have the same DNA at birth. Sometimes one twin develops a disease and the other does not. Comparing the twins' DNA at different times in their lives can be useful. Scientists can use what they find to get a better idea of the role of different genes.

Usually many sets of identical twins are studied. Some are raised together and some apart. If both identical twins have a similar medical problem, but are raised in different families, this is a strong sign that the disease may be genetic. If the problem happens to only one twin, even when the twins are brought up in the same home, researchers look for other reasons. The reasons are more likely to be environmental.

This is true of the disease rheumatoid arthritis. People with this disease have swollen and painful joints all over their body. Often only one twin will develop this disease. Researchers can compare the DNA of both twins and see where changes have occurred.

In this village, one in ten births results in identical twins.

In the Lab

Where in the World?
Having identical twins is not inherited; it happens spontaneously. Normally one in 300 births are identical twins. That is, except in one small village in India. In Mohammad Pur Umri, India, one in ten births results in identical twins. Scientists are flocking to the tiny village to take DNA samples. They are trying to figure out if there is a genetic reason.

N

Jagmmanpur
Rampura
Umri   Kuthaund   Kanpur   To Kanpur
MADHYA PRADESH
Gohan
Madhogarh   Hadrukh
Gopalpura
Bangra
Babai
Rendhar
Churkhi
Nadigaon
Aunta   Usargaon
Khanuwan
Mau   Itaura
ORAI
Kailiya   Kadaura
Air Khas   Betwa
Jhansi
Kusmilia
Pirauna
LEGEND
Saidnagar   Kotra   Hamirpur
To Jhansi

LEGEND
- - - State Boundary
.... District Boundary
——— National Highway
——— Major Road
——*—— Rail Line
● District Headquaters
● Other Town
~ River

Map not to Scale

Junk DNA

As researchers began looking into the mysteries of genomes, they noticed something odd. Not all the DNA is transcribed into RNA and sent to the ribosomes. In fact, only about two percent of our three billion base pairs become code for proteins. In between the genes are long stretches of other base pairs. At first, they didn't seem to have a purpose. Researchers named this kind of DNA **junk DNA**.

The amount of junk DNA is one of the reasons some genomes are so much larger than others. Certain organisms have many more non-coding sections than others. At first, scientists believed non-coding DNA was just taking up space. They thought it might be made of leftover genes that were no longer needed.

Some of the junk DNA is exactly the same as some viruses. One early theory was that most of the non-coding DNA was the leftovers from virus attacks over the centuries.

Ninety-eight percent of DNA is junk DNA.

Lately, researchers have noticed that junk DNA is sometimes used by the cell. This RNA doesn't become a protein. Yet it somehow regulates how and when a protein is made. Scientists have begun to wonder if the junk DNA is not junk at all. It is a mystery that scientists are still working on.

Researchers recently found about 500 stretches of human DNA that match the DNA in mice and rats. It's clear that we share quite a bit of junk DNA with rodents. So why does nature keep so much junk DNA in storage in animals? Maybe this DNA is not in storage at all. Perhaps it has an important job to do.

Not a Chance!
Each person's pattern of junk DNA is unique except for identical twins who share the same DNA. To identify someone, researchers use 13 locations along the person's genome. When comparing one location on one genome with the same spot on another genome, the chances are one in 45 that there is a match. Chances are one in 45 even if the genomes aren't from the same person. The chances of three spots matching are one in 157,000. The odds of matching all 13 locations are one in 53 quintillion!

Humans share junk DNA with rodents.

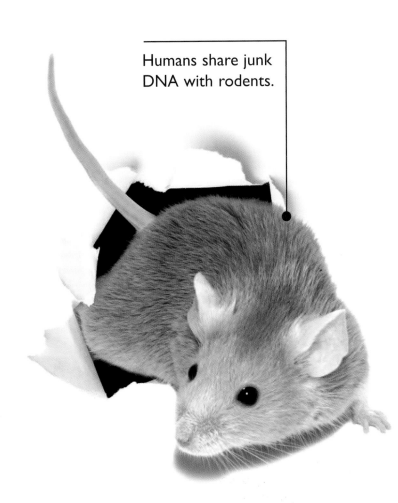

Chapter 5

DNA in Our Lives

Although we still do not know all the real functions of non-coding DNA, researchers have found an important use for it. It is the best way to identify people.

Because so much of our genetic code is the same, our genes are not a good way to tell us apart. Junk DNA is very different from person to person, however. In non-coding DNA are sections that repeat the same bit of code over and over again. They are called **short tandem repeats** or STRs.

DNA is an important tool in crime investigations.

Normal junk DNA might look like this: TCAT GCCA TTCG GGCC AATG.

A repeating section might look like this: TCAT TCAT TCAT TCAT TCAT.

Everyone's STR map looks different. In order to locate STRs on a person's chromosomes, scientists make a DNA fingerprint. Only a small sample of DNA is needed, such as the root of one strand of hair. After the DNA is removed from the cell, it is broken into pieces using a special enzyme. The pieces are lined up according to size on a nylon sheet. Radioactive dyes are used to mark the STRs. When finished, a DNA fingerprint looks a little like a bar code!

DNA profiling can be used to identify bodies after a tragedy such as a plane crash, to discover members of a family tree, and to study genetic diseases.

In the lab, scientists sort out DNA samples to identify people.

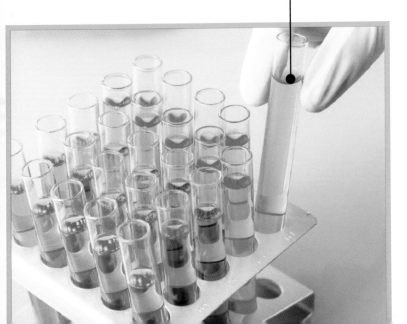

Mystery Solved
In a famous case, a woman claimed to be Grand Duchess Anastasia of Russia, daughter of Tsar Nicholas II. The Russian royal family had been killed during a revolt. Yet the woman said she had escaped. After her death, scientists used her DNA to prove that she was not the tsar's daughter.

Forensic Genetics

Buying and selling rare and endangered animals is big business. It is the biggest international criminal activity next to the drug trade. Birds of prey such as the peregrine falcon are popular targets. People steal eggs from the nests of wild birds. They smuggle the eggs out of the country in specially designed jackets. The jackets have up to 20 pouches where the eggs are hidden. That way the eggs will not show up on x-rays in airports.

The peregrine falcon is a target for smugglers.

DNA investigators are helping to catch these criminals. Using DNA technology, they can trace the parents of the hatchlings. If the DNA shows that certain birds were not bred in captivity, it proves the birds were stolen from the wild. With this proof, investigators can arrest the dealers and put them out of business.

Certain animals are prized for their skins or shells. **Forensic** analysts test the DNA in leather shoes, boots, and handbags. They want to make sure it is not from endangered or protected species such as caimans. They can also test exotic powders. That way they can make sure the powders do not contain ingredients from endangered animals such as the black rhinoceros.

Investigators are also on the hunt for poachers. They test the DNA of blood found at the scene of an illegal hunt. They compare that DNA to the meat in a suspected poacher's freezer or skins hanging on the poacher's walls.

Investigators check that leather is not made from endangered animals.

In the Lab

Ancient Mysteries
DNA is helping to unravel some of our oldest mysteries. In Egypt, the DNA of a mummy in a dusty tomb has been examined. Researchers are trying to prove that she is Queen Hatshepsut. The queen was one of the most powerful rulers of Egypt. Scientists have compared the mummy's tooth to the DNA of a known ancestor of Queen Hatshepsut. Scientists are almost certain the mummy is the lost queen.

DNA and Crime

One of the most important uses of DNA profiling is to solve crimes. Sometimes criminals do not leave items or fingerprints behind. If there are no witnesses it is hard to prove someone is guilty.

This is no longer the case. The courts now accept DNA fingerprints as evidence. This has opened up a whole new section of police work. Forensic investigators search crime scenes. They study suspects' possessions to find the smallest clues to solve crimes.

Even one tiny cell from the human body can give investigators the information they need. The root of one human hair or one drop of blood can give a criminal away. So can a skin cell or a bit of saliva. It all contains DNA. Suspects can be forced to give a DNA sample by law. Then investigators try matching the DNA found at the crime scene or on a weapon with the sample from their suspect. Finding proof that a suspect was at the crime scene or used the weapon can lead to an arrest.

The forensics used in police work can also help historians reveal truths about the past.

DNA profiling cannot only prove someone is guilty, it can also prove someone is innocent. So far, more than 200 people who were in prison have been proven innocent thanks to DNA.

In the Lab

Up Close

CODIS stands for *Combined DNA Index System*. It is a computer database of DNA profiles. When someone is found guilty, his or her profile is entered into the system. It is the largest DNA database in the world. The database has over six million offender profiles. A crime investigator can take the DNA sample from a crime scene and compare it to every other profile on record. The database has already helped police find 80,000 matches.

CODIS is a computer database.

Where Do We Go from Here?

Our understanding of DNA and genetics is growing every day. Researchers are figuring out how the hidden code affects our lives.

Being able to mix genes from different species is already changing how we eat and live. The ability to control DNA has given us new crops, including plants that produce more food. Researchers have created plants that help clean up poisons in our environment. Scientists have been able to raise healthier livestock.

Some people think we should not alter DNA and genetic material, however. They fear we may produce something bad for our health or the health of our environment. Working with DNA is a balancing act for scientists.

Is there a way to build a better forest?

They have to learn how to harness the power of DNA without causing problems in our world. Scientists are working hard to identify gene mutations that cause deformities and disabilities. They are also searching for genes or groups of genes that trigger diseases. One day we might be able to cure diseases such as Alzheimer's, diabetes, or cystic fibrosis.

In the future we might also discover sections of DNA that contribute to someone's turning to crime. We may be able to find the DNA that leads to drug addiction or other destructive behaviors. With the code of life unlocked, there is no telling what mysteries we can solve.

In the Lab

On the Run
The lowland gorilla is struggling to survive in the modern world. These creatures are shy, so it has been hard to help them. Now, DNA from bits of fur help scientists track the animals' movements. Scientists examine gorillas that died in order to trace family groups and monitor the gorillas for diseases. It will help researchers protect the endangered animals.

Notebook

Extract DNA from a Strawberry

Materials:
- Plastic container
- One heavy-duty Baggie that locks
- One strawberry (fresh or frozen and thawed)
- 1.5 ounces (44 ml) liquid dishwashing detergent
- 1/2 ounce (15 g) salt
- 32 ounces (950 ml) water
- Cheesecloth or coffee filter
- Test tube
- Glass rod or straw
- Ice-cold rubbing alcohol

Method:
1. In the container, mix detergent, salt, and water.
2. Place one strawberry in the Baggie.
3. Smash strawberry with fist for two minutes.
4. Add 1/5 of detergent mix to the bag.
5. Smash again for one minute.
6. Filter using cheesecloth or a coffee filter through a funnel into a test tube.
7. Holding the test tube at an angle, slowly pour the ice-cold alcohol into the tube until the test tube is half full.
8. Watch the DNA come out of the solution and float to the top.
9. You may try spooling the DNA on your glass rod or straw.

For Further Information

Books

Butterfield, Moira. **21st-Century Science: Genetics.** London: Franklin Watts, 2002.

Johnson, Rebecca L. **Microquests: Amazing DNA.** Minneapolis: Millbrook Press, 2008.

Simpson, Kathleen. **National Geographic Investigates: Genetics**. Washington, D.C.: National Geographic Society, 2008.

Web Sites

www.dnaftb.org/1/concept/

www.ornl.gov/sci/techresources/Human_Genome/project/info.shtm

http://publications.nigms.nih.gov/structlife/chapter1.html

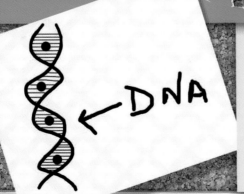

quote

"Science and everyday life cannot and should not be separated."

Rosalind Franklin
(1920–1958, English biophysicist)

Glossary

amino acids Building blocks for protein

antibodies Proteins in the blood that detect and destroy invaders

atoms Tiny particles

bacteria Single-cell organisms that are found everywhere and sometimes cause diseases

bases The chemicals that make up the rungs of DNA

chromosomes Long coiled threads of DNA containing genes

codons Groups of three bases that are the recipe for a specific amino acid

collagen Main protein in skin, tendons, bone, and other tissues

crystals Solids made of atoms in a specific pattern

cytoplasm Jelly-like material in the cell outside of the nucleus

deoxyribonucleic acid (DNA) A long strand of genetic information found in the cell's nucleus

enzymes Proteins that start or speed up chemical reactions

evolved Made gradual genetic changes over time

forensic Using science or technology to find facts or evidence for court

genes Sections of chromosomes that code for a certain protein

genome The total genetic information for an organism

helix A special coil shape

hemoglobin The protein in red blood cells that carries oxygen

insertion Something added

insulin Hormone that helps the body use sugar

junk DNA The sections of chromosomes in between genes that do not code for proteins

keratin The protein that is the main ingredient in things such as hair, feathers, and scales

membranes Thin, strong, bendable tissues

microbes Tiny, simple forms of life, such as bacteria

molecules Groups of atoms

mutations Changes in DNA

nuclein Early name for the nucleus

nucleus Control center of a plant or animal cell

protein Long chain of amino acids

replication Making an exact copy of DNA

reversal When something has turned around the opposite way

ribonucleic acid (RNA) The molecule that takes genetic information from the nucleus to the ribosomes

ribosomes Structures in the cell which make proteins

short tandem repeats (STRs) Small sections of DNA that repeat over and over again

species Group of plants or animals that are similar and can interbreed

spontaneous mutations Changes in DNA that happen for no reason at all

template Pattern

transcription Copying information from DNA to mRNA

virus Microbe that is much smaller than bacteria and causes diseases

Index